Rant.
Chant.
Chisme.

Rant.
Chant.
Chisme.

Amalia Ortiz

San Antonio, Texas
2015

First Edition

ISBN: 978-1-60940-444-4 (paperback original)

E-books:

ePub: 978-1-60940-445-1
Mobipocket/Kindle: 978-1-60940-446-8
Library PDF: 978-1-60940-447-5

Wings Press
627 E. Guenther
San Antonio, Texas 78210
Phone/fax: (210) 271-7805
On-line catalogue and ordering:
www.wingspress.com

Wings Press books are distributed to the trade by
Independent Publishers Group
www.ipgbook.com

Library of Congress Cataloging-in-Publication Data:

Ortiz, Amalia.
[Poems. Selections]
Rant.Chant.Chisme. / Amalia Ortiz.
pages cm
ISBN 978-1-60940-444-4 (pbk. : alk. paper) -- ISBN 978-1-
60940-445-1 (e-pub ebook) -- ISBN 978-1-60940-446-8
(mobipocket/kindle ebook) -- ISBN 978-1-60940-447-5 (library
pdf)
I. Title.
PS3615.R8215A6 2015
811'.6--dc23

2015008630

For all the Ortiz storytellers.
Thanks for all the chisme.

Contents

Magic Valley Girl

me acuerdo	2
these hands which have never picked cotton	5
Pinta	10
Chocante	13
jog past a South Texas field	16
a river, a bridge, a wall	18
Lullaby for the Immigrant Ocelot	20
Old Colossus, Resurrected	22
Eight-liners	23
How to Ignore a Wall	26
Reconstructing Skeletons in La Feria, Texas	29
Down Home	30

Mujer de Tacolandia

100 Words About 10 Music Legends	32
VIA Bus Bingo	33
Girl Strolls Down Nogalitos Street	37
Botellos	38
the night Ram died	41
tu love es no good	45
Colors	47
Community Garden	50
Amor Peligroso	52
Metáphora Tejana	54

Mestizo American

Jazz Babies   56
I'm Gonna Buy Me a Gun   59
Farming with the King   61
Grade School Fag Hag   63
Mosh Pit Pantoum   67
Weed Break   69
The Boulevard   72
spoken word is my temple   74

Madre Valiente y sus Hijas

The Women of Juárez   80
the short skirt speaks   84
Cat Calls   88
La Matadora   91
Do Not Go Silent   95
Some Days   96
Devil at the Dance   101
These Events   102
Unnamed   105
Unsung Lullaby   107

Acknowledgments   113
About the Author   117

Magic Valley Girl

me acuerdo

I remember tanto
de mi primer hogar
la tierra, el aire, el mar
                    I recall
me acuerdo details
of a place called home
however far I roam from those roads
                    me acuerdo

moments I remember
like tiny sparks and smoking embers
reignite flames once tamed
like so many names almost forgotten
but then I remember

me acuerdo de Noe and Doe-Doe
Bene, Flaco and Turbo,
Mimi, Bebe, Leti, Nefy, Meme and Esme
la Blanca y la Negra
Chena, Chon, y Chata
y la Hope who hated being named Esperanza
Tano, Tino, Mando, Delfino
and the locker room graffiti reading
Fina es muy fea
and Ninfa is a nympho!
                    me acuerdo

I remember tanto
de mi primer hogar

la tierra, el aire, el mar
                    I recall

me acuerdo details
of a place called home
however far I roam from those roads
                    me acuerdo

however far I roam, soy Tejana
can never forget my illicit language
fierce like Pancho Villa
my lengua so feared it was outlawed
from Texas school yards and halls, y'all
so, ten cuidado!
speak your Spanglish there
and they'll smack your manos

like my tia Tina
once upon a time they tried to keep her in line
in el Valle del Rio Grande
she was paddled for her covert
Castilian conversations
with every lick, her curses grew
they didn't know what she was saying
but what she meant, I know those cabrones knew
                    and I remember

I remember tanto
de mi primer hogar
la tierra, el aire, el mar
                    I recall
me acuerdo details
of a place called home

however far I roam from those roads
                    me acuerdo

my lengua is struggle
un víbora caught in the mouth of an aguila
ripped from its roots, it hisses and spits its history
from behind fangs ready to strike at any enemy

my language is Tex-Mex to the max
a photo-negative del otro lado
there they speak Norteño   here Tejano

my rasquache linguistics mix
Selena with Los Sex Pistols
like a dyslexic DJ
ready to bidi bidi   bomb the suburbs
punk ruka style
como los old-school roqueros
Ritchie Valens and Freddy Fender didn't care about the rules
'cause *It's your happiness that matters most of all.*

I remember tanto
de mi primer hogar
la tierra, el aire, el mar
              I recall
me acuerdo details
of a place called home
however far I roam from those roads
                 me acuerdo

these hands which have never picked cotton

my father unexpectedly pulled the car to the side of the interstate
and ordered his four children out into the cotton field
confused, we set down our video games
and flipped off the headphones
following reluctantly

he said, you've never picked cotton
you have no idea what it's like
it looks so soft, but it has thorns
which cut at the fingers even through gloves

we mortified teens reached down
with sideways glances embarrassed by the passing cars
plucked tiny clouds while rolling eyes
swallow a hand full of humble
but the real lesson would not be digested until years later

they say the first generation sacrifices
so that the second generation can achieve
only for the third generation to squander
and these third generation hands
these hands have never picked cotton

these hands, which have never picked cotton
softer than father's or grandfather's
these hands have never felt the prick of burrs
scrape deep, draw blood

these fruitless hands, which have never plucked grapes from the vine
are strangers to orange groves and grapefruit rows

these fragile knuckles have never scraped over washboards
or scrubbed floors for money
but have been caressed by abuela who did so in my place

these hands, which have spent more hours pushing buttons
than planting
with these fingertips
tender as abuelo's whispers
uncalloused as the fulfillment of grandmother's wishes

tender as this back, which has never ached in labor
never felt the sun baked flesh stretched beyond endurance
never known struggle as synonymous with sunrise
this body may not know, but must never forget

these hands, which have never worked leather
hammered heels, yanked soles, repaired saddles
sanded and polished shoes
grampa did, so that I may not

they say the first generation sacrifices
the second generation achieves
for the third generation to squander
and these third generation hands need to find purpose
these empty hands hold so much promise
these hands, which have never picked cotton

this body
the bones, muscle, youth not yet sacrificed to feed children
this body understands struggle builds character
but is still searching for what these hands will build

these selfish hands
these lazy, delicate hands

assimilated american made
these idle devil's playthings
play dead as if incapable of growing, crafting sculpting
a new america with these hands

these hands, which have never loaded weapons
these eyes, which have never stared war and death in the face
spared by dad's tour of duty
claim all these things I've never done
the softness of this body feels dad's scars
etched someplace on the skin of my soul

these legs, which have never hiked foreign jungles
are these legs so untested
that they will be the first generation not able to support their own weight?
will they buckle only to lay around and lounge?
was that abuelo's goal
moving to this land of 3rd, 4th, 5th generations
where what comes easily goes unesteemed
as these hands cover the ignorantly bored yawn of privilege

these hands, which have never picked cotton
become more american at rest
softer, dumber
their long-term memory loss bashing that next generation of immigrants
who dare aspire to my luxury of laziness

resting on
these feet, which have never walked factory floors
spent more time marching in protest than harvesting produce
these clumsy hands
more hours in libraries than in labor
in classrooms than cleaning public bathrooms

more toys than tools
more theory than action

these grateful hands write words of hope
of remembering and being remembered
give back this gift
scratch feeble offerings
to those who came before

these hands
these reverent hands grapple to fold together the past and the present
like hands folding in prayer
in the tradition of my abuela, bisabuela, tatarabuela
pray to their same god my modern concerns
to remember and be remembered

these feet stand on shoulders
reach down not to pick cotton
but to pull up the next generation
these words are for you
to remember and be remembered
to give and receive opportunity

these hands, which have never picked cotton, are ready
to park the car at the side of the road
snap the children out of their stupor
and into the fields
to appreciate the art of craft
of digging in the earth as creators

if struggle breeds character and sloth a deadly sin
then I am either the harvest my ancestors cultivated
or their sacrifices sinfully squandered

they say the first generation sacrifices
the second achieves
for the third to squander
and these third generation hands which have never picked cotton
these obligated hands are not my own

Pinta

Tia Irma gave Pinta to Gramma when she moved. Off
went Irma with her husband, three kids, and a dog.
But no cat— no Pinta.

Tia Irma called her *Patches*, but *Pahr-chess* came out
when Gramma tried to say it. The little cat was pintada
como un patchwork quilt. *¡Gatita Pinta!* Gramma
renamed her, and Gramma handed her to me.

Pinta is a girl's best friend. We share chicarrones—
stuff ourselves with them— until one of us throws up,
(usually Pinta) but that won't stop the two of us from
skipping down the calle to the tortilleria for more.

The Easter before Grampa died, Gramma said fifth grade
means boys will come too soon. Too old for the baskets!
Too old for the candy! Too old for the egg hunts! Besides,
she didn't have time— not with Grampa in the hospital.

But Tio Ruperto went behind her back and bought a basket
bigger than any I had ever had before! Gramma was so mad!
But I loved my uncle— more than I loved that beautiful basket
filled with color and flavor. I vowed I would save it forever.

Now two years later, Pinta comes along, and I rig my
last Easter basket to a rope, place Pinta safely inside,
climb the tree out back, and hoist my best friend, Pinta,

up the tree with me. Every weekend, we hide up there,
listen to the radio, and wait for people to pass
down the unpaved alley behind my house.

And with Pinta and my last Easter basket it doesn't matter
that Gramma doesn't allow other kids over.

With Pinta and my last Easter basket it doesn't matter
that I am only allowed to play out back   alone

With Pinta and my last Easter basket it doesn't matter
that Gramma thinks about boys more than I do.

That girls in the seventh grade don't climb trees or play
with cats like I do. Girls at school on Monday mornings
will chatter excitedly about

boys

boys at skate parties— boys at group bowling dates
boys at outings I am never invited to anymore
because everyone knows Gramma would just say

No!

But with Pinta and my last Easter basket
in a niche between three decaying branches
I can sing   loudly,   bravely

louder than the shouts from beyond the grey
dusty screen door— old, angry ideas protesting
girls climbing trees   *¡Ya bájate!*

Just a little while longer, please, in the trees
with my last Easter basket and my gatita, Pinta.
My beautiful Pinta— my Tio Ruperto later sells when
he is supposed to be cat sitting one summer vacation.

I am told a rich lady admired her unusual markings.
(more likely, she was hit by a car) Ruperto shoves
crumpled bills into my hand, but I do not count them.
Today Tio is Judas, and I will never be Peter.

My brother Bene never lets me forget Pinta every
time we eat tamales. He like to see me cry when he
jokes that whoever really bought Pinta made tamales
out of her. I force-feed myself tamales. Bene meows.

Chocante

chocante, shocking, startling, strange,
chocante, scandalous, sin vergüenza— without shame
chocante, shocking, startling, strange,
Abuela called me chocante so often,
I thought chocante was my name.

"Chocante" means unpleasant.
It's true. I'm not out to please.
"Chocar" means to collide or to crash violently.
¡Me chocas! Feel a head-on collision at the very sight of me.
"Cante." I sang.   "Canto." I sing.

  ¡Chocante!

Too loud! Abuela said.
You want way too much attention!
(too much for a Mejicana
adhering to convention)

Abuela taught me to be docile,
told me *girls are born to suffer!*
to cook and clean, not be obscene—
Serve the man first at supper!

  ¡Que chocante!

Yes, Abuela is now rolling in her grave.
Mujer muy mal hablada,
did you not learn to behave?

Señorita miss behaving
Señorita miss speaking
Señorita chocante, what husband
will tolerate that shrieking?

Cállate nena cochina.
Quédate en la cocina.
bocona, hocicona
mouth too big for una niña

raunchy, risqué arrastrada
pariah parrandera
Now, I'm persona non grata.
Perhaps, they should have named me Chata.

    Chatafuckup!

chocante, shocking, startling, strange,
chocante, scandalous, sin vergüenza— without shame
chocante, shocking, startling, strange,
Abuela called me chocante so often,
I thought chocante was my name.

chocante, chocante,   cho, cho
"Choad" is a short dick.
chocante, chocante,   cho, cho
"Chocha" is a woman's slit.
cante cante
       Can't chant cunt!
cante cante
       Can't cant smut!

I should close my pussy lips.
I can't get off on masturbation.

Feed my babies with my tits,
and save the goods for procreation.

Chose virgen or choose puta.
Can't exist as paradox.
Sex, class, race, and education
serve to keep me in a box.

I'm as subtle as machismo,
which is always in my face.
Oh, but I'm the one who has a problem.
I'm the one who's out of place.

choke, choke, choco—   ¡Muy chocante!
Abuela said it was an omen.
"Huerca chueca" means I'm twisted—
not attractive for a woman.

Been called angry 'cause I'm vocal—
Yes, I sure can talk a riot.
Been called angry, but I'm happier
than when I was afraid and quiet.

If you're proud and loud and willful,
you're "una mujer desgraciada."
But a matriarch must first rule herself,
y a mí nadie me manda.

chocante, shocking, startling, strange,
chocante, scandalous, sin vergüenza— without shame
chocante, shocking, startling, strange,
Abuela called me chocante so often,   I believed her.
Perhaps, she's the one to blame.

jog past a South Texas field

(ka^1) listen (ka^*) Chavela Vargas' death rattle (ka^*) the sound of my space Joaquin (ka^*) a shuffle of the Cantinflas guarache (ka^*) of eternity (ka^*) the cry of the stillborn child of lost traditions (ka^*) not your Sodoku (ka^*) not your Sphinx riddle not your Rubik's cube to twist (ka^*) not your token perhaps not yours at all (ka^*) but a pulga pedigreed perra (ka^*) loved no less by familia (ka^*) a placazo in raulrsalinas' mind jail (ka^*) not all times without ego (ka^*) not another ego sacrificed (ka^*) by a long-suffering Latina (ka^*)

I listen (ka^*) and I see you (ka^*) New Combes Highway field (ka^*) unsung until now (ka^*) I feel your humid heat (ka^*) these, your fifteen minutes (ka^*) not parceled (ka^*) you are not all fields (ka^*) not the oil field plundered (ka^*) off La Brea north of Ladera Heights (ka^*) I saw you too! (ka^*) wild teat fenced off and milked (ka^*) encased in your cement corset (ka^*) poor field! I knew you (ka^*) now I see you (ka^*) New Combes Highway field (ka^*) I run your length (ka^*) listen and hear you (ka^*) like words of a long (ka^*) forgotten ranchera (ka^*) *la rama del mesquite* (ka^*) *igual que yo se muere* (ka^*) forgive me, Grampa (ka^*) I never called you abuelo (ka^*)

(ka^*) without adjectives you are not (ka^*) littered, thirsty, or ignored (ka^*) attributes erased like non-European facial features (ka^*) airbrushed or whittled away (ka^*) no I hear your wide (ka^*) angled nose exhale (ka^*) your squat, diabetic limbs (ka^*) twisting in the wind (ka^*) I hear the choir of your (ka^*) seraphim crickets and (ka^*) cherubim crows (ka^*) feel the taunt of your (ka^*) mosquito minions (ka^*)

my decay comes daily (*ka**) revives with Lydia Mendoza's (*ka**) cannibal corpse (*ka**) with the roadkill (*ka**) on New Combes Highway (*ka**) hear it in the gasp (*ka**) between pez y (*ka**) pescado (*ka**) in the sound where air touches flames (*ka**) in the smell of the sage smudge return (*ka**) (*ka**)

(*ka**) in the cities it is easier (*ka**) to ignore (*ka**) but in the country (*ka**) where an army of sorghum stands at attention (*ka**) in rows like sun rays (*ka**) emanating out from the horizon (*ka**) in the field on New Combes Highway (*ka**) there is only growth (*ka**) or death (*ka**) (*ka**) (*ka**)

---

1. pronounced on the inhale as an audible sound

a river, a bridge, a wall

down by the river, the bridge, the wall
a heavy mosquito cloud drones on the severed resaca finger
such a tiny mouth for such a notorious rio
split like the cracked sidewalk where the VTC ends
coast guard, la migra, ICE, policía, DEA, never enough

down by the river, the bridge, the wall
hungry hands wave begging hats beneath the puente
ignored as a faded roadside shrine under caliche road headlights
no football temple floodlights sprouted in overgrown fields
where Friday night mobs foam feral like dog packs of dusty colonias

down by the river, the bridge, the wall
church ruins wilt on an old Indian trail and a cemetery's high grass
hides a forgotten historic battle marker as unadorned as
the palm bent in envy toward the huisache's painted white base
en el otro lado a neon dentista illuminates bootleg street vendors

down by the river, the bridge, the wall
winter Texans and spring breakers don't carry passports
cartels and coyotes don't pack papers

those are my bones buried deep beneath the border linea

un grillo canta solo
un grillo canta solo

the tangelo orchard
holds mute witness

the Lipan Apache, Kickapoo, Tigua, and Karankawa
weep with amputated arm extended
sign legal documents with feather and blood
sign legal documents with river reed and mud

down by the river, the bridge, the wall
there is no more time for nostalgic poetry

Lullaby for the Immigrant Ocelot

O mother cat
come race again by my side

your abandoned kitten
anticipates the continuance of your truncated lessons
slashed short by the blade of a wall
standing deadly like a cleaver stuck in meat

I lie in wait for you
here
in the brush shade by the river

my dignified companions
a number of confused creatures
parted from kin like seas at Moses' feet
the jaguar and roadrunner
the tortoise and antelope

they keep me company
here
by the guillotine fence

I mark the time
until you are ready to cross over and join me
then, we will munch on lizards and roam the endless night
I will rest my head once more
upon your spotted back
and coil in your warmth
our slick mounds gently rising and falling
in unison

we will slumber together
here
in the brush shade by the river

y me arrullarás hasta que me duerma

for we all drift into sleep curled tight like a fetus
then, when dreams unfurl
we fan out like fists unclasped
or flags stretched long on the horizon

y me arrullarás hasta que me duerma

Old Colossus, Resurrected

> *The wretched refuse of your teeming shore.*
> *Send these, the homeless, tempest-tost to me...*
> —Emma Lazarus, from "The New Colossus"

What brazen giant disturbs our Mother of Exiles?
Whose conquering limbs have freed her enlightening torch?
Is her imprisoned lightning extinguished,
her beacon breached, her silent invitation revoked,
replaced with tempests thrashing the trespassing masses?

What Leviathan lurks at Lady Liberty's golden gates,
not unlike Goya's *El Coloso* with warring fists drawn
and eyes shut against its own blind violence?
Which brutish Behemoth roused by her world-wide welcome
now arrests her tranquil harbor, her huddling homeless?

El Pueblo named the occupying darkness El Pánico,
this monster relishing the fruit of Sacco and Vanzetti,
excreting a spoiled, redacted myth of Ellis Island,
and scattering to the seven seas and four winds
the banished Mother and her dispossessed children.

Eight-liners

I. Esme

When her mother's social security check arrives, Esme sits Doña Lupe
down with her favorite dvd of El Chavo and asks her to keep an eye
on the boys. But Little Frank and Patricio have instructions of their own.
Stay in the house. Play on the computer. Call me on my cell phone only
if it is an emergency. Check on Buela Lupe every half-hour until she falls
asleep. If Buela asks, tell her Mamá is out selling Mary Kay. But please,
do not mention las maquinitas to her. Esme repeats this. Do not mention
las maquinitas to her. Buela believes those machines are not "of God."

II. Martín

Tio Rogelio goes to the triple seven to recruit bets on his football pots
and to sell his DVDs. Sometimes when Tia Nana se siente bien she makes
tamales para vender también. He lets me go along with him on Saturday
and Sunday nights even though he don't let me go in. So, I have to stay
in the van with the side door open, and when the customers come in and out
I yell "DVDs," show them our printed menu, or pop a disc in the portable
player if they want to check the quality. Tio says next year, when I am 16
he will trade with me, and I will get to go inside with the cooler of tamales.

III. Scribe

after reports of significant negative economic and criminal impact
after home invasions, armed robberies, after drugs, after prostitution
after cartel money laundering, racketeering, bribes-for-legal favors,
after a soft gaming control, after the quiet sanction of illegal operations,
after years of law enforcement looking the other way, after extortion
after selling the seized machines back to their previous owners, after,
after conviction of former state District Judge Abel C. Limas, after debt,
after addiction, after, why now after, now "Operation Bishop," only after

IV. Itzel

First, they came and took the computer— its empty spot on the desk a neat
dust-free square. The living room set went next. I kinda knew it was too
good to be true when they delivered it last year. The same day it disappeared,
we got a new sofa…well not new, but, you know…a thrift store replacement.
The flat screen went missing last, one day when I was at school. Then, the living
room was so quiet it didn't need any furniture anymore. Now, I just kick it
with Mauricio across the street. At first, he laughed at me, but I reminded him
that half of the stuff in his house his parents bought with Flexi Compras too.

V. Prescription

Diagnosis: malignant operation profit, operation investor, operation vender,
operation owner, operation landlord, operation manager, operation gaming,
operation underground casino, and operation poverty. Precautions: metastasis
of operation fake store-fronts, operation gaming homes, operation crime, and
operation corrupt officials. Pre-operative consideration: While no cartels have
been named in arrests, police believe the money is too large for cartels to keep
away. Recommended treatment: surgical removal through operation cite patrons,
operation closure, operation arrest, and operation seizure. Prognosis: unknown.

VI. La Paca

Me encantan las maquinitas, las luces, el ruido, la música, y la compañía,
their electric chirps of encouragement and alarms of celebration, their
colorful glowing fruit, bells, diamonds, and triple sevens. Mis ojos scan
the 8 betting lines for matches—3 horizontal, 3 vertical, and 2 diagonal.
Mi favorita is the one with los gatos because it reminds me de todos los
gatitos que hang out in my neighbor Samuel's yard. I once got a jackpot
on a gato machine. So now, if I see one que tiene gatitos, that's where I
sit for at least an hour. Sí, me encantan, y I feel lucky tonight, real lucky.

VII. Script

After an 18 month investigation under the direction of Homeland Security,
state and federal law enforcement agencies are working day and night
to close illegal eight-liner establishments in Cameron County. There are still

currently 200 gaming businesses in operation in the county, and authorities say they're not done yet. According to Cameron County District Attorney Luis Saenz, the name of the crackdown, "Operation Bishop," originated from a call the bishop made expressing concern for how eight-liners were effecting poor. The Diocese neither confirms nor denies the name's origin.

VIII. Doña Paca

Doña Paca was arrested during a raid, but she still visits las maquinitas. The charges were dropped, and she got away with a warning that next time they could fine her up to $300. She thanks God she had her papeles. She saw the fear on some of the faces arrested and surely deported. She leaves the county now, and when she can convince her comadre Sandra to go with her, las viudas drive to Laredo. There, las maquinitas are as plentiful as un-harvested pecans on the ground. She still prefers los gatos, and sits patiently for at least an hour whenever she finds one. They make her feel lucky, she says, real lucky.

How to Ignore a Wall

Avoid maps. Tell yourself the
Earth is flat and the wall keeps
U.S. citizens from falling
off of the end of the world.
or

It is like a space suit equalizing
pressure and protecting life.
To proceed without it would
suck the country into a vacuum.

On the restless river, justice
drowns in the current and
conscience flip flops on the
banks like fish in the sun.
If you plug your nose you
can ignore the stench but...

how to ignore a wall?

Count the martyrs like sheep
until they lull you to sleep.
Stack statistics like bricks
and aid in its construction.

It is rude to lurk in doorways
so like a vampire, ask permission
to enter, but if permission is denied
what to do with those who enter anyway
like the bold arms of a hurricane?

How to reason with nature?

And how to ignore a wall?

Try risking nothing.
Look up to the palm tree tops.
Look down across the sugar cane and cotton.
Look anywhere, but do not make direct eye contact
with the wall, or if you must, stand so close
that the eyes blur and you no longer see it.

Keep calm and just keep eating.
Don't ask where your food comes from
or who picks or prepares it—
about Monsanto,
about how the rich got rich,
or who the gatekeepers are.

Do not look up the words
social or *justice* in the dictionary.

No, if you are a writer, write about something
else. For your career's sake, write about anything
else. Tell yourself you are powerless to
change anything, and then do not express
those feelings of powerlessness in your writing.

Ignore class, but chase the dollar.
If you have brown skin, convince
yourself you don't. If you have
indigenous blood, bury that
fact like broken treaty artifacts.
If you have fair skin, why think

about race at all? Tell yourself you
live in a post-racial America.

Tell yourself political poetry is passé.
That identity politics is a thing of the 60s.
Tell yourself the only good art is esoteric and
consider yourself part of that elite.

And then when injustices do occur, avoid
them too. Tell yourself Trayvon has nothing
to do with a wall. Oscar Grant happened a
world away. People of color are not all related.
Tell yourself it is someone else's problem.
Use words like *ghettoize* and *self-victimization*
to describe any writer who tries to shame you.

If you have the power to print this, don't.
Befriend a cartel. You might as well.

If a steel wall accidentally cuts you in
two you better learn to live a broken life.
Accept mutilation as normal.
Stop counting the abuses,
unless like counting sheep
They lull you into a comfortable,
air-conditioned sleep.

How to ignore a wall?
No, really I am asking you,
because it seems to me
somehow most people do.

Reconstructing Skeletons in La Feria, Texas

(for Viridiana)

Down Villarreal Street, she traces migration trails door to
door searching for proof. Here, a sympathetic señora lifts
a fingerprint—a phone number for the son of a dead man
fabled to have owned her building. Maybe he remembers names

and dates. Evidence and skin impressions dull with time like a
once-sharp edge of familiarity. A tune seeps out from
a vaguely reminiscent cantina husk. Past railroad tracks,
a panadería hermit crab claims the discarded shell

of a drive-thru Texaco. Down on Main, glossy signage and
fluorescent lights exorcise cobwebbed shadows of a childhood
home. The past is a frail document crumbling in careless hands.
Smoke and history belong to the victors and forensic

scientists. The proof she seeks escaped on a rare breeze through small
cracks in the wall like 60,000 dreams of children scattered.
She's convinced if she can clutch on to one single memory—
a movement, a taste, or a twinge of nerve impulses— she will

render words like "illegal" and "America" meaningless.
Until then, her senses testify in confirmation and
inadmissible chills. The river changing course reminds her
not even the Earth has a thing to hold onto on its ride.

Down Home

Down by the river, Texas ends and begins
Down by the river, sun blisters the skin
& when coyotes come crossing the patience wears thin

Down on the delta, la migra demands proof
Down on the delta, textbooks rewrite the truth
& cartels keep supplying new jobs for the youth

Down on the rancho, trocas tower over cars
Down on the rancho, son cantinas, not bars
& on channel five Tim Smith rolls his Rs

Down in the colonias, outdoor showers lack heat
Down in the colonias, dogs roam dusty streets
& primitos chase a soccer ball on bare feet

Down in the valley, the big river divides
Down in the valley, metal and rock collide
& one root splits and flowers on both sides

Mujer de Tacolandia

Sir Doug knew how to party, celebrating life with song.
Augie Meyers flavored keyboards with Mex and acordeónes with Tex.
Flaco's skinny fingers fly— through borders, over land and time.
Baldemar Huerta learned to translate his longing into Freddy Fender.
The crying sky made Stevie Ray Vaughn's guitar weep along.
The accordion played Esteban Jordan, not the other way around.
Lydia Mendoza's music lives on in the lark's border song.
A witch hunt ran Janis Joplin out of Port Arthur.
The best huracán to hit el Valle was Narciso Martínez.
Queen Selena's flower was plucked too soon but still blooms.

VIA Bus Bingo

San Antonio
 downtown daily
 young and old alike
gather 'round bus benches on the corner
of Soledad and Commerce Street
 everyone anticipating that moment of winning

 VIA bus bingo

68, 68! Please, God give me a 68, 68!
 Damn! 82.
Hey, what number are you waiting for?

    Pues, el number 3 pa'l centro park moll.

a group of preppy pink tourists
drowning in a sea of brown faces
excitedly steps on to a trolley headed
west towards that quaint little market
square where they will purchase
authentic Mexican mementos like
 ceramic chili pepper hotplates
 or clay Aztec calendars

annoyed by their perkiness
Celia, miss teen hoochie,
 smacks her gum
 rolls her eyes
 and turns to eye

through the Payless Shoe Store window
a pair of higher-than-high-heeled shoes
        a perfect match for her shorter-than-short shorts
she counts her bills and the minutes
calculating if she can pick up a pair
without missing the number 92

just then Willie from Victory Temple
spots her stack—
        of cash that is
and makes a play for the green with a—

Care to help out your brothers in need at the Young Men's Victory Shelter?

        Bingo!
number 92 arrives
and 'ol Maestro Martínez
salutes his fellow veteranos
and hobbles in line
        cane leading the way
        hat, coat, slacks, and shoes impeccably
        pressed, polished and primped
        way into their fiftieth year of usage

Now that's class, vavoso!

Lil' Alfie hollers hopping out onto the street
he high fives his homeboy, Hector,
and pockets the seven digits he just scored
off some fine ass hyna on the number 84

number 84
        Bingo!

a new group of winners lines up single file
to trade places with a new group of players
        waiting to trade sun and sweat
        for air conditioned seats

and all day long Willie from Victory Temple
trades handshakes for Bible tracts
and *fuck-offs* for *God-bless-yous*

all of a sudden
        Bingo!

Conchita
        (or should we say Conchota)
and her grocery bags
spill off the number 97 and all over the sidewalk
        two other large and wrinkled ladies
        scramble to help Concha regain her groceries
                and her dignity

        unnoticed,
a bum leaning against the Payless window
quietly pockets an apple

Concha plops down next to the women
in a tight fit on one of the benches
        searches through her bags
        and produces a small box of Church's Fried Chicken
¿No quieren un bis-que-te? she offers
while Hector and Lil' Alfie
roll on out of the dollar store
        sporting new shades and
        matching dangling chain wallets
Check it out man, number 68!

Bingo!

and they slide on out of the humid heat
     way on into the very last seat of that number 68
     that snakes its way west down Commerce Street into the sunset
left on Frio Street where students exit right in front of UTSA
Stuck-ups! Hector grumbles
and the bus cuts right on through to Guadalupe Street

at the Alazan Apache Courts
     some of the nation's oldest public housing
Lil' Alfie rings the bell

Bingo!

next stop, Guadalupe and Brazos
where the six o'clock mass bells
of Our Lady de Guadalupe
welcome him home

Girl Strolls Down Nogalitos Street

for Jacquie on Taft

Girl must be walking to a beat in her head
'cause her metronome hips make music
Abuelitas frown as she passes
waist playin' bass as her heels drum the pavement
Can't really blame her though
Girl can't help it
This city just sings through her

Botellos

public places of the poor/are rarely pleasant/corners where the
destitute congregate/resting areas designated as appropriate/
deemed least offensive/for tired, hungry, and other undesirables to
gather/are not meant to be pleasant/most places/we are not even
welcome to wait/sometimes there simply is no place for us

public places of the poor/are not meant to be pleasant/we are rel-
egated to bus stops and parks/huddle under overpasses/holed up
near rivers/snap to the advantages of air-conditioned libraries/but
mostly wait/bide the time in so many lines/life on hold/awaiting/
soup or employment/housing or medicine/or sometimes agonize
over access/to what is rightfully ours

as is often the case at Botellos Community Check Cashing/a
last chance stop for/owners of overdrawn accounts/like a prize
fighter/delivering knock-outs/in empty-handed blows

i have stood among them/the hand to mouth/working-class
down-and-out/shuffling forward/eyes bowed/heads humbled/like
visitors to the Virgin de San Juan/who martyr themselves for/
God/dragging their bodies on bloodied knees

here, hands turn over and over/the promise of salvation/not found
in rosary beads/but the prospect of prayers answered /if only
someone would cash/a tiny piece of paper

sooner or later, money turns all of us religious/has us down on
our knees bargaining/for a better interest rate/on our mortgaged
dreams

Botellos Community Check Cashing/saves more souls than the Guadalupe cathedral/down the street/seals more futures with a Judas kiss/for lifesaving silver/here, more prayers are uttered beneath breath/more crosses drawn on furrowed brows/than checks cashed

here, sinners made of saints/giving into the temptation/meager earnings squandered on beer/wine/cigarettes/Phillies blunt cigars/overpriced bread and eggs/wilted produce/and peanuts by the cupful/filler lacking nutrition/passed off as food

i have stood among them/these my people/christening bills with tears/the ones without the luxury of budgeting/when the only thing that separates us/from the 6th night in a row/of potatoes for dinner/is a man behind Plexiglas

like a bookie/he only stands to profit from loss/has seen too many people lose it all/to show emotion/so he stacks and stamps/counts and collects/returns and rejects/and begins again/always with the same word/Next!/ to him, hearts drop as easily as pennies/into the take one, leave one tin

here, we walk among angels/working miracles with money orders/ for those del otro lado/angeles pagando cuentas like playing numbers/$50 en la luz/$50 en el teléfono/$10 para el agua/$20 para un tarjeta telefónica to send home/$30 guardado for groceries/and a 20 oz. of Tecate/everything else goes to Western Union

public places of the poor/are rarely pleasant/corners where the destitute congregate/resting areas designated as appropriate/ deemed least offensive/for tired, hungry, and other undesirables to gather/are not meant to be pleasant/most places/we are not even welcome to wait/sometimes there simply is no place for us except places like Botellos Community Check Cashing/so, here we wait patiently/for our luck to change/and the pendulum swing/to rock back and forth/between despair and the prospect of hope

the night Ram died

*Ramiro 'Ram' Ayala, whose iconic bar Taco Land became an
institution for underground music for more than three decades, was
shot to death early Friday in a possible robbery attempt, police said.*

— John Tedesco, Jim Beal and Mary Moreno,
San Antonio Express-News, online (06/25/2005)

the city burned hot and humid
in sticky, sweaty celebration
the night that Ram died

the night Ram died
1,000,000 lungs
exhaled whoops and
howls-at-the-moon
into the San Anto skyline

downtown, a traffic jam honked a horn concerto
heard all the way to Alamo Heights
the beat of bass bumped bumper-to-bumper
in gridlock automobile standstill
amid 1,000,000 patas on the pavement
parading in puro pinche pachanga parranda
in true San Antonio style

the night Ram died
San Anto was drunk on another Spurs championship
intoxication stumbling stranger into embracing stranger
violating public drunkenness, open container, liquor laws
and creating uncontrolled crowd dangers
while wheelie poppin' motorcycle cops looked the other way

the night that Ram died
was like some Tejano holiday
raza invented
like wrapping New Year's inside Cinco de Mayo
and sprinkling two weeks of Fiesta on top

but Ram
a crusty old loud-talkin' man
wasn't one of those 1,000,000 fans
Fuck the Spurs!
Ram of beer and barflies
Ram of pool hustlers and punk rockers

Ram was behind the helm of Taco Land
and Taco Land was a dive bar
on the river near old factories and warehouses
no touristy river walk pretension there
only the cinder block shell
of a no frills ice house
wallpapered three layers thick with rock iconography
graffiti, flyers, and band bumper-stickers

a few busted vinyl booths, a pool table
and a kickass jukebox full of records
as old as the backed up plumbing
in the ladies room where every gal
sprawled in a shaky spider stance
over the clogged toilet

and, oh lord!
it's hard to pee when the walls won't stop moving
uncountable nights spent spewing
vomitous into the river

at Taco Land
on any given night
Ram peddled dollar Lone Stars
and sucked swigs off his mystery hooch two liter
opening his stage
to guitars growling
alcohol attitudes
and ass-whipping elbows thrown to the furious beat
of rock and roll rebellion
fueled by Ram's belligerent rants of
 Don't be a pussy!

on nights thick with dope smoke
overheated kids hung on the patio
praying for a breeze to blow
from the muddy river banks down below
there hobo river rats
rested serene on cardboard pallets
or sometimes waited to sleep under a picnic bench on the patio
once last call was hollered and the party moved elsewhere

'cause this was a home away from home
to many homeless and boozers
to the rockers and losers
freaks and fans
shady hookers and bands
on any given night at Taco Land

the night Ram died
the streets were alive with 1,000,000 joyous cries
but as San Anto partied
the music died with a gunshot

petty thieves killed the man behind the bar

but not the legend

the Dead Milkmen immortalized
the local music scene canonized

the shrine of over thirty years of South Texas punk rock history

the night Ram died
you might as well have buried the pyramid with the man
or set him aflame atop his building
a pyre burning on the river
their ashes as inseparable as their legacy
untimely extinguished
like a cigarette butt savagely crushed beneath a biker boot

the night Ram died,
1,000,000 souls
shouted to the heavens in unison
where one can imagine his soul joined the celebration
of 1,000,000 voices victorious

tu love es no good

tu love es like
that station wagon I crashed way back when
I could have tried to fix it
pero ya pa' que?
sin aseguro
no sirve
es basura
tu love es no good

como Wranglers sin Ropers
no vale la pena
tu love es no good

tu love es como cruising the drag on pata
dressed in drag
or como riding over the haunted railroad tracks on a bike
or como searching for the donkey lady alone
or como Walter Mercado
your love me asusta
for the reels, babydoll
damn
no good
no good

nombre dude, tu love es
como los Dallas Cowboys cada season
como los Lakers sin Kobe
como Kobe with a minor

tu love no tiene vergüenza
no good
no good

tu love is like a night in county
it steals my dignity
and sticks it to my culo
te sales
no good
no good

como un port a potty the last day of a street fiesta
todo cagado
y apestoso
no good
no good

eres tan mala con migo
babydoll, you're so mean
if I tried to sell your love at the pulga
it would only be good para three things

pa' nada
pa' nada
y pa' nada
no good
no good

Colors

someone tried to steal the colors of the Westside
tried to lock people behind gray walls
like walking the institutional halls of a gray future
black barred windows
penned in like prisoners
uniforming children like inmates
in khaki and white
someone tried to steal the colors of the Westside
tried to steal its pride

someone tried to steal the colors of the Westside
in government issued homes
and forget government-backed student loans
cause' the only schools these students are predestined for are reform
someone tried to steal the colors of the Westside
somebody lied
somebody said
separate but equal
and forgot the rainbow does not end
where there are no pots of gold to spend

someone tried to steal the colors of the Westside
but the Westside snatched them back
in the bold bombs of taggers
spray painting midnight blue warnings to outsiders
separating us from them
separating boys from men
with graffiti covered daily by the Chinese shop owner
who reclaims his colors by out-cussing those little culos
in his own brand of broken Spanglish

someone tried to steal the colors of the Westside
tried to steal them from kids
locked into step
like they were in lockdown
kids who steal their colors back when no one is looking
hide them behind their backs
breaking rules in violent attack
sagging those khaki slacks
flashing boxers, chones, and sometimes crack

and before you say it's wrong
when you see that fourteen year old girl flashing thong
ask yourself where you would be
if your colors were stolen from you
leaving you alone to tend a colorless home
where your only chance at change
is changing diapers
the pinks and baby blues
the I've-got-to-get-the-hell-out-of-here hues of those
nothing-else-to-do-with-my-life blues

someone tried to steal the colors of the Westside
but the Westside snatched them back
in the roses, violets, and plátano yellows
of plastic hot house flowers
and candles of every pigment guarded by saints
on altares tended daily like bougainvillea and gardens by our elders

and the most colorful mother of them all
the Virgen de Guadalupe
protects her mosaic iridescence
in every cathedral, corner store, mural,
and forearm tattoo

placas purchased in pain and blood
scream, *Fuck the marines!*
These colors don't bleed.

someone tried to steal the colors of the Westside
but the Westside fought back
in the sandía red swirls of sangre
from afternoon chingazos
bad blood and beer spilled over
quién sabe qué
outside icehouses
where the only thing colder than the beer
are the cold stares at you if
you're not from here

whoever tried to steal the colors of the Westside
tried to paint it ghetto gray
but this is not the ghetto
here on the Westside
because here on the Westside
is where our colors thrive

Community Garden

They planted the seeds
together   when they were just lovers—
newly launched satellites finding parallel orbits
circling their love.

Their first harvest
(overabundant—
cucumbers and squash long as a forearm
sage, rosemary, and Serrano peppers
tomatoes by the dozen) they

roasted into sauces,
ate their fill, and fed
family and friends.

But when their two paths became so synchronous
they collided   into one,
a different seed was planted,
and they found themselves   forever
tethered to one another
hurtling along an unexpected path
a nine month countdown to their new family. Lovers

became husband and wife,
and the best-laid-plans were scrapped for survival
better jobs,
a wedding,
doctor visits,
and preparations.

The garden was the first item left
    off the to-do list.
Watering slipped the mind.
Not enough hands to weed…
She could not bend in the sun in the heat.

Shame at the sight of
the garden's fallen glory made them both give   up hope,
and neglect it completely...

But during our despedida the other day,
she waved from her air conditioned nest on the sofa
as he walked me out worried about his coming harvest
It's a girl! he confessed as
we crossed through the front yard

past the overgrown,   sun-scorched tangle of green
wild sun-flowers now towering
over the ruin.

Sharing our goodbyes and best-laid-plans,
we shook hands before a cluster of orange
caught his vacant gaze   into the unknown future
infant tomatoes hanging from the vine
He dove into the wild to discover
a whole plant pregnant with Serrano peppers
I haven't even watered these!

Hands dug into the unplanned,
and extracted a bundle   of fresh sage and Serranos
a handful
extended in friendship
an offering to feed me
on my way home.

Amor Peligroso

Watchale!

You, with that Big Red in your brown hand!
El doctor dice que será mi muerte.
Bad for my alta presión y the cause
of my diabetes con su caffeine
y corn syrup. Te pone bien loco!
Ten cuidado y think before you drink!

Pues, it's too late for me. Since the tender age
of three, mi Mami had me hooked licking
sticky liquido by the lenguaful
de mi tetera— red coating my tongue.
I had no idea the sweat treat in
my tummy would someday cost me my teeth.

¡De veras! ¡Soy adicta! Now my heart
pumps saccharine sangre. And I'm told if I
don't say adios it could cost me my toes
like my Tia Toña whose sweet tooth took
her big toes in exchange for a lifetime
of munching Butterfinger y Baby Ruth.

This is more than addiction. This is love-
in all its self-destruction. ¡Amor peligroso!
¡Amor podoroso! Si fue posible,
I'd say the drink gave me ojo—with that
mysterious taste, hard to define taste ...
like liquid bubble gum, or like pop-rocks,

like nada natural ... Pues, it tastes red.
redder than the fruit of the prickly pear
redder than juice of the Ruby Red
red like el diablo who made and cursed it
Te embruja, and will not release you
from its spell until it takes your toes!

Watchale!

Metáphora Tejana

soy un dicho in nine sílabas
comforting colita de rana
amor de pendejos consejos
Rebel optimist? ¡Sí se puede!
herencia of wisdom casera
tiny pearl cultured from mi pueblo
lost in translation agudeza
provincial, pero valid, porque
Cada cabeza es un mundo.

Mestizo American

Jazz Babies

I poison tiny dreams
with Coltrane's "Favorite Things"
    at naptime
I preside over
10 sleeping rug rats
lying on 10 plastic mats
and I play DJ
laying down the soundtrack
to infant fantasies   my class

10 toddlers between the ages of 1 and 2
during awake hours
    they waddle, they toddle
    they teeter, they wobble
        and they do fall down
        cry, fight, scream, bite,   learn

but from the hours of noon to 2
they snooze
and while other classes slumber to softer sounds of
    Rock a bye baby, on the treetop ...
though my students are sleeping
the lessons don't stop

see, I poison tiny dreams
with Coltrane's "Favorite Things"

I give the gift of the off-beat
the syncopated rhythms of the unusual
because reality seldom happens

to the beat we plan
    or the key we orchestrate
it sneaks up and pops us
with a bang
like the unpredictable nature of pure jazz

I teach them
life will throw you some surprises, babies
but if you just roll with it
you will never miss a beat

and when Coltrane turns music into madness
I admit I worry a little
hover over
wanting to be there for them
if that savage sax growl grows
into a force they must fight
in the land of the dreaming
the musical landscape I introduce is bumpy
    but safe
no drumbeat too dangerous
no horn too hazardous
no baby battles that don't return to the
    raindrops on roses and whiskers on kittens

this music is not too complex
for their unconscious apprehension
for the lesson jazz teaches is life

I wonder what
wee make-believe dramas unfold in baby dreamscapes
    tumbling teddies
    dancing dogs
    tap-dancing turtles

and when Coltrane blows chaos
    trilling moans
    and groaning tones
when Coltrane gives up control
their small psyches take over
    unblemished by adult bitterness
    free from fully-grown fear

when Coltrane gives up control
I wonder if only virgin ears can truly hear
    the untainted sound
      of freedom

so yes, I poison tiny dreams
with Coltrane's "Favorite Things"
more than likely, the music
    and I
will have no lasting effect on their lives
but if only for a while
maybe
    just maybe
every slumbering baby
lived free like jazz

I'm Gonna Buy Me a Gun

a hymn

Well, I woke up to read all the headlines today.
And I never would've guessed it would end up this way,
'cause I prayed it would stop when they shot M.L.K.
Oh Lord! I'm gonna buy me a gun!

Now, the line at the gun shop is straight out the door
And they say if they sell out they're ordering more
Before guests at the White House include Michael Moore!
Oh Lord! I'm gonna buy me a gun!

I'm gonna buy me a gun and shine it up well,
'cause this here whole country's 'a goin' ta hell!
Gonna defend ma family from Satan's black spell.
Oh Lord! I'm gonna buy me a gun!

Now, you're better off holding "a bird in the hand"
Than believin' a dreamer just three-fifths a man.
And I swear on the Bible, and not the Koran!
Oh Lord! I'm gonna buy me a gun!

Now, the flood gates are open. It's all gone astray.
And the next thing you know all our neighbors are gay!
That kinda change isn't coming if I get my say!
Oh Lord! I'm gonna buy me a gun!

I'm gonna buy me a gun and shine it up well,
'cause this here whole country's 'a goin' ta hell!
Gonna defend the White House from Satan's black spell.
Oh Lord! I'm gonna buy me a gun!

I'm gonna buy me a gun and shine it up well,
'Cause this here whole country's 'a goin' ta hell!
Gonna defend ma homeland from Satan's black spell.
Oh Lord! I'm gonna buy me a gun!
Oh dear Lord! I'm gonna buy me a gun!

Farming with the King

Being Elvis is costly.

Maybe not at first. At first, all it takes is a striking resemblance, some pomade, and a few rockabilly shirts. After Tio Rocky found Jesus, he gave up his alcoholic ways, stopped running with gangs, left the Rio Grande Valley, and raised a family of Bible thumpers on a farm outside Mattoon, Illinois. Cousin Gladys met Reese at Vacation Bible School the summer before her senior year. She found his piercing blue-eyed stare irresistible.

Being Elvis is costly.

Everything is vintage: 1950s suits, skinny ties, patent leather gators, military uniform. Shortly after they were married, Reese started lip syncing at a local bar. The couple ran a small organic farm not far from Tio Rocky's. On weekends, they traveled to farmers' markets to sell their produce. Everyone in the family got a kick when Elvis would show up at barbecues, quinceañeras, and weddings. Things got strange—strained even—when Reese didn't dial it down for funerals.

Being Elvis is costly.

Comebacks are expensive: leather and gold lamé suits, rings, chains, and huge sunglasses. He began to truly believe he was king—stopped responding to his own name even. He never dropped the act. Elvis went everywhere eliciting Elvis-level commotions at the supermarket, church, and the post office. By the time Reese had aged into his cape-wearing phase, he was touring his show every weekend leaving Cousin Gladys to sell at farmers' markets alone. All of his Elvis money he reinvested in Elvis: weekly hair salon appointments, custom made rhinestone suits, memorabilia, and an old 1950s Cadillac convertible on the front lawn in various stages of restoration. You can't be the king on a farm. There would be no Elvis sightings of him working the field. Elvis did what any king would do; give orders to the peasants from his throne.

Being Elvis is costly.

The highest price Reese paid was his family. Cousin Gladys drew the line at fat Elvis—an absentee father in his own home. She sold the farm, paid off their debt, and moved back in with Tio. Reese Jr.'s sneer and hip sway wowed at family reunions for years after.

Grade School Fag Hag

I was a teenage fag hag
all my teen crushes
were gay
George Michael
gay
Boy George
gay
Morrissey and Michael Stipe
        bisexual?
with that definite gay vibe

the prettier the man
the harder I fell

but if I dig deeper retrospect reveals
before I was even aware of my own nature
I was a grade school fag hag
3rd grade
my best friend Brian Waterhouse
gay

didn't know it then
but like my teen crushes
time explains a hell of a lot

Brian was
well?
one of the girls

boys hated him
hated his grace
his loose waist, hips, and wrists
his giggle
his sensitivity
all qualities I loved
and defended with fists
on the playground
defended with pride

until
the school wide talent show

a drama queen's dream
any kid with a talent
could skip study skills
to rehearse

Brian went to work on a modern dance piece
my talent—stand-up comedy
for two weeks I studied old Redd Foxx albums
while Brian twisted and turned
to the count of
1 -2 -3 -4
and 5 and 6 and 7 and 8

the prettier he moved
the harder I fell

until
the morning of the talent show
the show wasn't scheduled until late afternoon
but Brian wore his costume that morning

his 3-piece lamé Liberache's-pride-and-joy frock
some colors should never be worn by straight white males

Brian was wearing all of them

orange off the shoulder blouse
purple *Hammer Please Don't Hurt 'Em* pants
gold floppy beret
accentuated with a single sassy purple plume
and had he permed his hair?
students and teachers whispered

I
avoided him
unable to look him in the eye
for some strange uncomfortable reason
my 3rd grade person lacked the knowledge to explain

backstage
I'm running lines
Brian is applying makeup
and my mind is made up
no more boy best friends
this hot flashing shame must end
things *must* be NORMAL again!

then the music began

> *"A place where nobody dared to go*
> *The love that we came to know*
> *They call it Xanadu..."*

he skipped
he shimmied

he pranced with pink triangle pride
he vogued before vogueing was vogue
everyone whispered
and I fell in love

in love with his freedom
and spent that afternoon
on the playground
defending freedom with fists
defending with pride

so now
when I hear some self-righteous son of a bitch
preaching that homosexuality is a perverted choice
I want to tell them about Brian Waterhouse
3rd grade
and ask why an innocent child would choose
to be hated

Mosh Pit Pantoum

Everybody's movin', everybody's movin',
everybody's movin' movin' movin' movin'..."
—Fugazi from "Waiting Room"

Speed up the tempo and, I'll throw an elbow,
shouting *Die fascist scum!* and *Fuck authority!*
when the chorus drops. Get out of my way
during the verses. I skank low and mean,

shouting *Die fascist scum!* and *Fuck authority!*
jabbing the air with angry sharpie exed fists.
During the verses, I skank low and mean,
stage dive off a speaker, and into the pit.

Jabbing the air with angry sharpie, ex-fisted
security catches a kid on the perimeter just about to
stage dive off a speaker, and into the pit.
Chuck Taylors slide across sweat drenched concrete.

Security catches a kid on the perimeter just about to
fall, and rises back up again with the next snare kick.
Chuck Taylors slide across sweat drenched concrete,
and pogo in place until the crowd opens up—

fall and rise back up again with the next snare kick.
The Betties holding up the wall lose balance
and pogo in place until the crowd opens up.
Docs stomp. A douchebag jock sucker punches.

A Betty holding up the wall loses balance,
slams the edge of the pit and spirals back out.

Docs stomp a douchebag jock's sucker punches.
Don't be that asshole. Aggression broods,

slams the edge of the pit and spirals back out.
Speed up the tempo and, I'll throw an elbow.
Don't be that asshole aggression broods.
When the chorus drops, get out of my way—

Weed Break

after noon
    after class
we cut cross campus
    cross the street
to the weed break spot
    "Smokin' Tree" empty lot

cross the street
to hang in shade of sweet mesquite

afternoon
    after class
sneakered feet
tramplin' sun burnt overgrown grass
    time to puff, puff
    pass the dutchie to the
    right hand side
our counter-clockwise
counter-cultural salute
our anti-institutionalization libation

professors and TAs
work inside this sun blessed day
    and we know that kind of life for us
    ain't too far away

but not today
    today it's 4:20 again

and we're not that suit
    still waiting
    for the percolating
    powdered bean
    watered caffeine
or the dean
    waiting for her fix
eyeing matches and her cancer sticks
or the secretary
    always running late
    no time to escape
        and meditate

what goes up must come down
and this lot
    this tree is my vacation
these friends are my relaxation
and this weed is my   meditation

what goes up must come down
    and it's 4:20 again
    time to puff, puff,
    pass the dutchie to the
    right hand side
      smile
          mile
             wide

among decaying
weed tree branches swaying
    like the hips
we later be layin'

scenting sheets with joy
    sweet sweat
    and spilt seed

horny, yes
but don't blame the weed
we need this break

ain't no mistake
we remain in full view
    not the safe thing to do
so our message comes through
    fuck you
    and you
    and…
you, you're ok
    …but fuck you

slow the pace
    stand back
    give some space
      chill
this is our time
our youth, yes
but adult enough to give
    and give and give
      but never take
fuck that

I need my weed break

The Boulevard

at 4 a.m. on Hollywood Boulevard near Vine,
when the gutters are cluttered with glossy
night club flyers, fast food trash, and random
castaway collections of those homeless now
huddled up to metal storefront grates locked
and pulled down tight for the night, as a sex
shop peepshow flashes a neon beacon, when
all frolicking at the Frolic Room has ceased,
when the trendy Hollywood scenesters have
all stumbled off into the dark to other scenes,

when each tourist-leaching t-shirt-and-trinket-
pusher has fled, and the busboys have rinsed
every last greasy spoon and bussed it home to
rest their American dreams in beds far from
Hollywood where the 4 a.m. silence betrays
the wild, frantic bustle of daylight sightseers
meandering like cattle grazing, hungry eyes
scanning the ground for more, more spectacle,
more gossip fuel for the celebrity fire, more
proof that this filthy boulevard is exceptional,

at 4 a.m. on Hollywood near Vine, when the
valets' ballet of cars has concluded, and there
are no buskers keeping time to rattling subway
rhythms, no big-business heels taping urgent
staccato marches, or Katsuya-spying paparazzi
clicking frenetic bebop tempos, when all the
bouncers have bounced on, then the only
sounds are the tired whispers of the guardians'
tongues, the paid caretakers—lot attendants,
porters, janitors, guards—standing dutiful vigil

at 4 a.m. on Hollywood Boulevard near Vine, a street cleaner ceremoniously shuffles, his arms swaying like a priest swinging incense, during this, his early morning ritual pressing steadily forward waving a pressure cleansing stream in a constant zigzagging pattern past the long-forgotten, fallen stars of Edward Dmytryk, Joel McCrea, and Mitchell Leisen. (Fans no longer pause for photos alongside Kathleen Lockhart, Marshall Neilan, or Mercedes McCambridge.)

at 4 a.m. on Hollywood Boulevard near Vine, the grime of the hard-luck hustlers and bleary-eyed beggars is swept away, and the struggle to outdo one another's hustle is temporarily on hold at this corner which tells time by traffic and marks seasons by wreathes on makeshift headstones later trampled underfoot by shit-stinking panhandlers and star-chasing dupes—each a deformed American tragedy reinforcing the mythology of the velvet rope, yes at 4 a.m.

this is as clean as these Hollywood streets get

spoken word is my temple

in the beginning there was the word,
and the word was with God,
the word was God,
and God was love
spoken word is love

L-O-V-E spelled out
far too frequently
mistreated
the word badly beaten
yet the sacred heart
of the word is still beating

in the beginning there was the word,
and the word was with God,
the word was God,
and God was love
spoken word is love

love is my temple
like the first word
because the first word was not
the great *I am*
the first
I think therefore I am.
No, it was something more like
the great *We*
or the great *We are not alone.*
or the great *I am also, and I understand*

as for any words before *We*
well, unheard words are worthless

and so it began
the great back and forth
our great exchange
impossible to embrace without the word

but
if God is love
and God has been perfected
and love as perfect as God
is placed in defected
hands of mortal man
does love share our fate
through pain is love transformed to hate
love
deformed
like the word mispronounced
misinterpreted
or forgotten

I come to this temple
searching for love and absolution
I come inside this temple
to escape retribution
I hide in this temple
to protect my weak constitution

spoken word is my temple
but sometimes words fail me
love leaves me hanging
impotent muscle in my mouth
flopping flaccidly

spoken word is my temple
but sometimes I commit blasphemy

and like all weak and weary
I give up hope
like all meek
or those consumed by fury
I give up hope

spoken word is my temple
but sometimes I lack humility
I hang myself
with self-pitying
ropes of redundant words
become unworthy of the word
convincing myself
it is not worthy of me

and then I am cursed

until I return to this church
and am baptized a-new in verse
a disciple of words
once lost but now found
speaking all tongues
of the tower of babble
yes, I am babbling
my Eucharist
reciting incantations of
Christ almighty connection

can you feel my words
you, my gods and goddesses
lost in this odyssey

we call the world
best experienced and heard
through each other

yes, my sisters and brothers
yes, I use you
to create a new gospel
we aren't used to
in a world that underestimates
the power of a smile and a simile
it's ancient prophecy
yea, though I walk through the
valley of the shadow of death
I will speak no evil
for spoken word is my temple

in the beginning there was the word,
and the word was with God,
and God was love
spoken word is love

the word is out
have you not heard
if you live by the pen
you must die by your words
and if God is the word
and if God is the word
then the Devil must be

silence

Madre Valiente y sus Hijas

The Women of Juárez

at the West tip of Texas
a line divides us from them
and on the other side
they all look like me
yet on my side we sit passively nearby
while the other side allows a slow genocide

500 missing women
some claim more
some less
some dismissed as runaways
against parents' protest
hundreds found dead
hundreds still missing
the exact count is a mystery
and those disappearing daily
they all look like me

I am a dead ringer
for an army of the dead
Mexico's slaughtered sisters
all slim, long dark hair, petite
some say pretty

all young
all lost
or dead
and they all look like me

some foolishly search for one serial killer
when bus and cab drivers
even cops are under suspicion
while the ever growing numbers reflect an entire society
where young women are expendable
young women like me

mothers recognize raped and mutilated remains
daughter's clothes with mismatched human bones
DNA that doesn't match
those are her shoes
but that's not her hat
this shirt is my sister's
but those aren't her slacks
dumped like trash
burnt to ash
in the desert that keeps its secrets
one body found dumped in the middle of the street
in a neighborhood not unlike mine
on my side of the line
where I am alive
and my father reclines
in his retired military easy-chair bliss
of Fort Bliss

Mom and Dad warn to be careful
but aren't overly concerned
when my brothers and I
cross the border from El Paso to Juárez
for late-night cheap college drink-a-thons
as long as we stay on the touristy paths
that may exploit
but do protect Americans and our American dreams

we are different
and even my parents don't seem to see
all those missing women
they all look like me

but I am told I am different
less Mexican, less poor
American thus worth more
different

yet all I can see are eerie similarities
they all worked like I do
so many last seen
going to or coming from work
at US corporate owned maquiladoras
but I'm told this isn't an American issue
and I'm lucky here on the safe side

safe
yet not quite out of earshot of distant cries
of families searching ditches and roadsides
bearing snapshot after snapshot
of my brown eyes

have you seen this girl?
she is my sister
¿la has visto?
es mi niña
my baby
mi hermana
my wife
have you seen her?
this face? ¿esta cara?

when you fit the profile of a predator's prey
you can't help but take the crimes personally

I am a symbol of those who survive.
mouth open in defiance of their silence
spared by a line in the sand
drawn between their grandfather
and mine
and if that line had fallen closer to home
somewhere between you and I
who would I be?
what would my worth be then?
and if silenced who would speak for me?

the short skirt speaks

for the Nuestras Voces 2011 National Conference,
the SlutWalk movement,
and for Shelly who testified the accuser "did not act like a victim"

she was told she was too angry
no hysterics
told she did not act like a victim
no tears
told she did not cry like a victim
no pleading
only angry accusations

but above all the he said/she said
some were deaf to her defense
some could only hear the resounding babble
of the short skirt which to some
speaks louder than truth

when the short skirt speaks
it will not be ignored
when the short skirt speaks
it holds credibility hostage
it brandishes a time bomb of shame
and carries with it a list of demands

the short skirt demands all eyes upon it
demands culpability
it provokes while placing blame
on women who were never
meant to wear the pants

the short skirt spits
bring me the mute victim's tongue
roasted over the fires of rape
bring me the presumed innocence of the accused
and I will multiply the burden of proof
as I rain down reasonable doubt
from way up above   on my high horse   side saddle
answering all suspicions at last
with the flash of one bare   thigh

short skirt says stop
short skirt says go
short skirt says stop
short skirt says go
stop
the short skirt did not say stop

oh, all the old wives are held captive by the tales of the day
when the short skirt opened up
all expectation of violence
for those who seek sex for pleasure

the short skirt whispers sexuality
too dangerous for the weaker sex
the short skirt scapegoats the body
and absolves all voyeur eyes
commanding this culture of victim-blaming
and oppression by slut-shaming

the short skirt speaks a dangerous myth of distraction

take a hypnotizing stare if you dare
up the short skirt and mysteriously forget
female feticide, dowry and honor killings

forget date and acquaintance rape
forget the sex slave trade
the short skirt will explain them all away
defining sexuality in male terms
and bringing at last
a bloody end to the word *feminism*

I was told I was too angry
no hysterics
told I did not act like a victim
no tears
told I did not cry like a victim
no pleading
only angry accusations

but above all the he said/she said
some were deaf to my defense
some could only hear the resounding babble
of the short skirt which to some
speaks louder than truth
truth which if heard
sounds something like this:

it did happen   I did not give consent
short skirt or snowsuit   it can happen to anyone
however I was dressed   it was not my fault   and now

I will not cry for you
I will not plead to convince you
I will not dress for you
I will not justify for you   because
this is how a slut walks

this is how a prude talks like
this is how a victim acts
this is what a survivor sounds like
this is what a feminist looks like
this is how Madonna rages and how the whore weeps

Cat Calls

hit me with one of those cat calls
see, I was walking down the street
like your sister
like your momma
walking down your street
like your daughter
like your gramma
composing a symphony in my mind
I could see the violinist about to touch the bow to the strings
when—
Damn, milk it did your body good!

I was walking down the street
like your sister
like your momma
walking down the street
like your daughter
like your gramma
but you don't want to hear that
'cause you're only cruising for a lover
so all you see
are curves

hit me with one of those cat calls
when I was walking down the street
composing a poem in my mind
I had written the outline
and was about to start the rhyme when—
Hey mami, where you headed?

and you saved me from the prison of my mind
call me mami again, please,

hit me with one of those cat calls
just one more time so that
I can feel my womanly worth
I'll call you papi, because
every woman really wants a daddy
and you're the first man ever
to be completely honest about
what women really need

I need another cat call
because I sometimes lose awareness of my curves
and you remind me
I should never worry my little head
about the problems of this man's world
because there are big, strong machos like you
who value your women
so much you just have to celebrate your sister's beauty with a
¡Ay sabrocita!

'cause I was walking down the street
like your sister
like your momma
walking down your street
like your daughter
like your gramma
feeling kind of scared
you know, walking down that street
in that neighborhood
in these times
and just as paranoia was kicking my ass
Whoa, beautiful, I'm in heaven!

you made me feel so at home
and even a little turned on to boot
hey, where are you going in such a big hurry
come back and give me another cat call
'cause nobody can howl like you, baby
gets me all hot just to wonder what else you can do
with that tongue wagging back and forth

you always remind me
it doesn't matter what I wear
all that matters is that I have what it takes
between the legs
'cause I'll be a complete mess and—
Honk! Honk! You fine!

what was I thinking
actually worrying
about things that don't concern me
like education and respect
when all I really need
more than flowers
more than candy
more than respect
is a hunk-a-hunk-a man in a hunk-a hunk-a car
and those drive-by love notes to convince me that
I think I'm in love too!

Hit me with one of those cat calls
you've finally hit on the one thing that
drives me wild
I just hope your daughter gets to meet
such giving men
as you

La Matadora

for Carmen Bermúdez

all eyes on her defiant pose
this moment the proof of her existence
she assures herself
    soy matadora

machos scoff between swigs of Presidente
    una mujer?
sure she will crumble like paper
beneath 800 pounds of ego charging
    brave but stupid

they wait in this concrete arena
packed to the rafters
to watch her failure
to witness idiotic dreams ripped to pieces
some stare in disgust at how surely
she enters the round strutting
los gallos will not crow the arrival of this sun

las damas don't know what to make of her
dressed in men's clothes
while they drown in oceans of fabric
some lean forward gripping their seats
while others ridicule, spit and hiss

la matadora proceeds forward focused
circles resolute in purpose
whips cape from shoulders
presents it, a curtain closed against the sun

stretches the unsubstantial shield
to the savage beast released

la valentina arches back, drops chin
raises shoulders and elbows to the sky
and begins the deadly dance
so like the pasodoble
spins and stomps hypnotizing with the wave of nimble hips
teases the animal forward
now what man does not believe her capable?
when her sex invented, perfected
the art of seductive movement

the two figures quickly fatigue
her foot slips in the dust
she catches the step, rotates
escapes with a leap and recovers
leaving el toro weary
indignant animal wet with sweat
fur grimy, matted

she readies herself
gathers her weapons
relaxes in her training
years of defiance have led her here
> *má-ta-lo má-ta-lo*

now convinced the crowd feeds her
> *má-ta-lo má-ta-lo*

but la matadora deaf to the wild crescendo
hears only her own heartbeat
slows it and steadies the hand
silences fears and directs the blade home

la matadora, picadora
chiquita pero picosa
raises slender swords
begins the sharp swipes and jabs
the first for Mother
another cut for the naysayers
and yet another blade stuck
for men who have raised fists against her sex
a stab for her blood, tears
a stab for loss, rebirth
her baptism of blood as matadora

má-ta-lo má-ta-lo

the beast now drunk with rage
does not see her sex
cannot distinguish male from female
sees only target, opponent
la matadora see only the challenge
drives deep and lands a stab for her sisters
whether they claim her or not
another for her unborn daughters for their future

the arena erupts
blood sport propelling all to their feet
woman warrior whispers a prayer of forgiveness
stares straight into exhausted eyes
reveres the hefty defeated mound before her

má-ta-lo má-ta-lo

and with expert ease aims an ultimate strike
hits the mark with a jerk and a wrench

for mercy she prays
mercy, in her failure the bull and the crowd would have denied

if a man fails to kill they call him woman
if a woman fails what do they call her?

saluting the heavens in her victory
la matadora can only wonder
the once fierce crowd
like the bull and her fear now conquered

Do Not Go Silent

a villanelle for survivors

To any ear that hears I'll cry!
My solace, that my voice is heard.
It did happen! No matter who denies!

Though he said/she said sensationalize—
Though gossips distort every word—
To any ear that hears I'll cry!

False friend—a wolf in sheep's disguise
Came creeping when the vision blurred.
It did happen! No matter who denies!

Brutal tracks covered with monstrous lies—
There is no proof of what occurred.
To any ear that hears I'll cry!

til justice does not pass me by—
Though reparation seems absurd—
It did happen! No matter who denies!

I'll shout 'til heaven itself replies!
Die vindicated, not unheard!
To any ear that hears I'll cry!
It did happen! No matter who denies!

Some Days

When people tell me I am a strong woman
I want to tell them
I don't always *feel* strong

some days
I get so tired of being strong
I want to let my legs collapse
under the weight
of the world
on these shoulders
and just cry myself to sleep

some days

some days
I get so tired of being strong
frustration sends me pacing the floor
     no solutions
     nowhere to go
     nothing to do but pace myself crazy

the women of my family have taught me
how to be strong

     they have also taught me
     how to despair

I watched
as Gramma stood for hours at a time
staring out beyond a dusty screen door

sighing such a defeated sound
as if to say
      this cannot be my life

I remember days
the walls closed in so close
she would pace back and forth
      pace back and forth
      pace back and forth
teaching the caged bird that
having the option to leave
doesn't make leaving any easier

some days
I get so tired of being strong
I want to run away

some days
sadness grips my heart so tight
      it hurts to breathe
      and it only helps if I grieve
in the manner the women of my family
have taught me

I want to be alone now
for what will follow
thankfully
the bathroom
my most reliable sanctuary
is indifferent to these episodes

I force the sadness to the surface with sound
squeeze out sounds

no self-respecting woman would make
in public

I push at the pain
induce a vomit of tears
as if despair was labor
and I could birth out of me
with every groan
  pang
  throb
my naked
  sorrow

I was taught well
how to purge my pain in private
pick myself up
off the wet tiled floor
  and mop away
  all evidence
  of anguish

and though to many
in our society
the image of a woman
  grieving
  alone
  slobbering like a child
is unattractive
to me it is an image of true strength

in my family
women
have embraced their pain

for generations
kicked back straight shots of grief
no chaser to help them past the bitterness
locked horns in a head on collision
with heartache
and survive
while many men in my family
           fear it
disguise it
      run from it
              dance around it
do anything to avoid it
displace pain with rage
punch dents in
        walls
        cars
        kids

let pain infect them
holding it in
scarring them inside
afraid to feel
heart break

being strong
doesn't always mean
feeling strong
some days
I get so tired of being strong
some days
I get so tired

I let go

some days
we must let ourselves fall apart
before we can move forward

Devil at the Dance

Her papá taught her to never look down.
A good dancer engages her partner's gaze
or trustfully rests an ear on a strong shoulder.
So, by the time she finally noticed   the hoof   the claw
tearing up the floor where shiny boots should be,
it was too late.

She was already in love.

These Events

(Inspired by events of 7-10-07)

My younger male cousin is a US soldier fighting in Iraq, while my elderly female cousin is in an immigrant prison camp in Raymondville, Texas. They share something in common. I wrote a poem about hundreds of women found raped and murdered in ciudad Juárez. In response, someone threatened to rape and murder me. These events all share something in common. I'm told this threat could be a stupid kid someplace on this planet playing with a keyboard and hate speech.

The officers suggest, *Think of it as something light and not dangerous.* Light, I think, like the attitudes toward the Juárez murders. Hundreds dead. A slow war against women a stupid kid someplace on this planet can make light of with a keyboard and hate speech. These events share something in common.

I reluctantly filed a police report. Reluctance due to *our political climate.* I wonder what microscope will now shine on me. But I'm a citizen! My elderly cousin would agree. She has lived in this country longer than air has lived in my lungs. Now, she is being held as an illegal in what amounts to a concentration camp. A tent city designed to detain families in the 100 degree South Texas heat. Excuse me if I'm a little paranoid about calling the police! The officer inquires, *Have you had any other hate speech aimed at you?* Yes, I answer, in this political climate. I write about Mexicans and immigrants. Yes, I answer, in this political climate, but speech is speech and this the first threat. These are paranoid times. You are either with us or against us. So, although my father was career military in two U.S. wars, and I was born in Virginia, I can't shake the fear which now makes me question calling the cops.

My younger male cousin is fighting in Iraq, while my elderly female cousin is held in a prison camp in Raymondville, Texas. I hold my grandfather's birth certificate in my left hand. My own certificate in my right. Fingers wrap the documents into fists and war with one another. One tells me my male cousin is the hero. The other, my elderly cousin is the threat. While angel and devil fight it out on my shoulders, I recognize these people share something in common. Halliburton profits from war. Halliburton profits from privatized detention camps and the prison industrial complex. There is money to be made by keeping tribes scared and scattered. These events share something in common. A common environment of fear and hate. Hate the insurgents. Hate the immigrants. You are either with us or against us. They say. Build a wall. Secure the borders. Post 9/11 U.S. never looked so much like Nazi Germany with barbed wire and fences. Mad scramble to secure papers and passports. A climate of fear and racism. These events share something in common. No longer history lessons we memorize callously. No longer headlines I can ignore with a quick click of the button, turn of the page...

I hold my grandfather's birth certificate in my left hand. My own in my right. For some time now, I've considered my future as a mother. Imagine going to Mexico when the belly grows round. Surround myself with women and a midwife. Dream of birthing a child of dual citizenship. A harmless dream of giving a child a continent rather than a single government. Let it choose where its allegiance lies. A return to the days when my ancestors roamed this land freely before the coming of the flags of New Spain and New England. When tribes followed seasons like flocks of birds. Drew life from the land. Followed the pickings like great brown waves rolling across this continent. The hunters and gatherers, the Toltec, the Olmec, the Coahuiltecan, Karankawa, Comanche and Apache, Purepechan and Huichol, Guachichiles. But even the Aztec turned a paranoid eye on its brown brother in the last days of its fading empire aiding the Spanish in war against the Chichimecas, who the Aztecs called the lineage of dogs. Brown turning on brown. These events share something in common.

My grandfather was born in Lagos de Moreno, Jalisco, Mexico, lakes of brown, and I am aware I come from brown waves rolling across this continent long before crossing a man-made line constituted a threat. I reluctantly filed a police report. The cops called it a "terror threat." And some place on this planet a stupid kid is playing with a keyboard and hate speech claiming I am the threat. And perhaps I am using the cards dealt to me—European tongue and education once beaten into burro Indios who refused to speak good English. Now these, my strongest weapons against another Wounded Knee, Trail of Tears, Tlatelolco, another Jim Crow, another Dred Scott Decision, another Auschwitz, Guantanamo, Abu Ghraib, Vietnam and Iraq, another Katrina, Juárez and Final Solution… These events share something in common. Besides my tears and prayers. These events share something in common.

Unnamed

The border crisis has a name. It is Cristal. Her name is Kiara.
The border crisis speaks Spanish so quickly, my rusty tongue is inept.
The crisis named Kelley has carried her son Peter all the way from
    Honduras.
The crisis is five years old. He is 3 years old. She is in her mid-twenties.
The crisis is two years old and learned to walk, but does not trust his
    own feet anymore.
The crisis does not trust being outside of a mother's embrace.
The crisis needs a shower. It has been 8 days. It has been 20 days.
It has been *God-knows-how-long* since the crisis has showered.
The border crisis has tiny dreadlocks beginning to form at the nape.

At the Sacred Heart church, everyone claps when the border crisis enters.
    Bien venidos. We welcome you.
    Now, tell us your name.

Overwhelmed by the border crisis,
I try to focus on what is controllable,
like two small girls in a portable shower stall.
The sisters, Cristal and Kiara, trust so easily,
I could wet their weary feet with my tears—
bow my head and offer my hair as an unworthy washcloth...
Overwhelmed by the border crisis,
I try to focus on what is controllable—
unfit am I to even be their Mary Magdalene
No room. Many will say.
Cast stones and spit. Turn the border crisis away.
Overwhelmed by the border crisis,
I try to focus on what is controllable

like dressing the little one quickly,
so Cristal is left with some privacy and dignity.

They asked me to give you a poem.
But, what you need is a bowl of soup.
They asked me to give you a poem.
But instead, I will fit you for shoes.
They asked me to give you a poem.
But, what you need is a shower and a bed.
They asked me to give you a poem.
But instead, I will comb out your hair, and paint your tiny nails.
They asked me to give you a poem.
But, what you need is a safe home.
They asked me to give you a poem.
But, all the talking in the world is not what you need.
So instead, I will stay quiet and listen
as you tell me your name.

Unsung Lullaby

hm aht sa ki-i-i-i
ko chit sa na-a-a-a
po keet sa na
po keet sa na

My husband learned an indigenous lullaby
volunteering in an Otomí orphanage.
Someday we will sing it to our child.

my little one
little rabbit
my little goat
my little goat

Sabato Rodia birthed the Watts Towers
raised them for 33 years on a foundation of steel, wire,
    and mortar
shaped the shattered and discarded
scraps of tile, pottery, seashells, and bits of colored glass
his Seussian mosaic spires grew nearly 100 feet high
lovingly brought up, patiently nurtured, and painfully
    protected

ingenious or insane

when asked why, the sculptor said,
"I had in mind to do something
big, and I did."

the Watts Towers:
Rodia conceived them, created them, then signed them over to
    someone else,
and disappeared

hm aht sa ki–i–i–i
po keet sa na–a–a–a
ohk chit sa na
ohk chit sa na

Mother, where are you?
I have spent years tracing the edges of your absence in my
    imagination.
Have you been building me the Watts Towers?
Pouring all your creative energy into
an inspirational monument
larger than life?

A testament to something so "big,"
my rabbit offering, a small price to pay?

my little one
my little goat
my little bird
my little bird

    estranged father to two sons and a daughter
    Sabato Rodia began building the Watts Towers
    after the collapse of his marriage
    seeking redemption from alcoholism and despair
    he obsessively handcrafted
    "Nuestro Pueblo" — "Our People"
    the largest structure ever made by one man alone
    "I did it all by myself. I never had a single helper."

ingenious or insane

when asked why, the sculptor said,
"Good, good, good or bad, bad, bad.
You be a half good and half no good, well that's no good."

three children and the Watts towers:
Rodia conceived them, created them, then signed them
          over to someone else
and disappeared

hm aht sa ki–i–i–i
ohk chit sa na–a–a–a
ko chit sa na
ko chit sa na

My child, I wasted years trying to build the Watts Towers
telling myself it was for "our people"
committing to anything other than you
to prove I could commit to something ...

(the unspoken fear — that I would change my mind
five years into your childhood
          that I would truly be my   mother's child
          that an urge to disappear would outweigh obligation)

forgive me my long-eschewed little goat
forgive me

my little one
my little bird
little rabbit
little rabbit

Mother, you once sent me a message
saying you want to meet me but   you are afraid.

Fear no more. Simply

    build me the Watts Towers.

Restore pride to your community
with nothing but shattered and discarded

Show me your life's "something big"
and history might forgive—
might resurrect
    your little rabbit
    your little goat
    your little bird.

    First, build me the Watts Towers, Mother. Then, tell me
    it was worth it.

hm aht sa ki–i–i–i
ko chit sa na–a–a–a
po keet sa na
po keet sa na

    My husband learned an indigenous lullaby
    volunteering in an Otomí orphanage.
    Someday we will sing it to our child.

Acknowledgments

Many thanks to the groups with which I have performed and toured including ¡Puro Slam!, the Chicano Messengers of Spoken Word, the Slam America Bus Tour, Def Poetry, Diva Diction, Women of Ill Repute: Refute!, Women Artistically Kollecting Experiencias—Unidas Prosperando, ColectivaSA, and MadMedia.

Thanks are also due to the countless organizations which have opened their doors to me including CantoMundo, Hedgebrook, The National Hispanic Cultural Center, The Guadalupe Cultural Arts Center, The National Performance Network, The National Association of Latino Arts and Culture, The National Poetry Slam, Talento Bilingüe de Houston, El Centro Su Teatro, SaySí, The Jump-Start Theatre, Urban 15, The Pantages Theatre, The Narciso Martinez Cultural Arts Center, The San Antonio Current, Mujeres Activas en Letras y Cambio Social, National Association of Chicana and Chicano Studies, The Alfredo Cisneros del Moral Foundation, The Valley International Poetry Festival, The University of Texas Pan American Creative Writing Program, and Centro para la Semilla.

Thank you Chris Wise, Emmy Perez, and Norma Cantu for the time and help you dedicated to this manuscript. Also, thanks to my editor Bryce Milligan.

There are simply too many individuals who have supported and encouraged my writing. These names represent only a fraction of my support system: Jorge Piña, Benjamin Ortiz Jr., Benjamin Ortiz Sr., Sr. Martha Ann Kirk, Retha Oliver, Shannon McGarvey, Joel Settles, Nicolas Valdez, Maria Ibarra, Jason "Shaggy" Gossard, Charles Peters, Gary Mex Glazner, Brenda Riojas-Nettles, Celina A. Gomez, Edward Vidaurre, Alan Oak, Craig Pennel, Sterling Houston, Trinidad Sánchez Jr., Jacqueline

Salame, Elijiah Rios, Dr. Brenda Risch, Elizabeth Mestnik and my EMAS cohort, Carmen Tafolla, Irma Ortiz-Widrick, the Widrick family, the Hinton-Stancil family, and the entire Ortiz familia for all the stories. Unending thanks go to my best reader and husband, Kip Austin Hinton.

Thank you Stan Lathan, Russell Simmons, and HBO for making so many of my dreams come true, and thank you to Michele Serros for paving the way.

Many thanks to all the editors for publishing the following poems:

The Line Between Us (Rethinking Schools): "The Women of Juárez"

Cinco de VIA, five years of Poetry on the Move: "Girl Strolls Down Nogalitos Street"

¡Juventud! Growing Up on the Border (VAO Publishing):"The Devil at the Dance" and "Pinta"

Along the River 2: More Voices from the Rio Grande (VAO Publishing): "Lullaby for the Immigrant Ocelot,""Amor Peligroso," and "These Hands Which Have Never Picked Cotton"

Boundless 2012: The anthology of the Rio Grande Valley International Poetry Festival (Art That Heals, Inc.): "Devil at the Dance," "A River, A Bridge, A Wall," and "Girl Strolls Down Nogalitos Street"

Chicana/Latina Studies: The Journal of MALCS: "Eight Liners"

Interstice (South Texas College Journal): "Unsung Lullaby" and "Down Home"

The Rio Grande Review (The University of Texas-El Paso): "La Matadora"

Hinchas de Poesia: a digital codex of contemporary pan-american writing, No. 12, online: "The Boulevard"

The Mas Tequila Review (Mas Tequila Press): "I'm Gonna Buy Me A Gun (a hymn)"

La Voz de Esperanza (Esperanza Peace and Justice Center): "Lullaby for the Immigrant Ocelot" and "The Women of Juárez"

The Monitor: "100 words about 10 Texas Music Legends" and "Farming with the King"

The Ultimate Poetry Boxing Championship (Poxo Publications and Coalition of New Chican@ Artists): "Punk Zazen"

Deportation Nation Literary Migrations (Red Calacarts Publications an Imprint of Calaca Press): "Old Colossus, Resurrected" and "These Events"

Poetry of the Lowest Common Denominator (Turtle Stew Productions): "Cat Calls"

About the Author

Originally from the small town of La Feria, Texas, Amalia Ortiz studied Creative Writing at the University of Texas-Pan American and now lives in Harlingen, Texas. During a Hedgebrook fellowship, she wrote her poetry musical, *Carmen de la Calle*. In 2014, she completed an IC3 residency at the National Hispanic Cultural Center in Albuquerque. She is also a recipient of the the Alfredo Cisneros Del Moral Fellowship.

Ortiz is widely known as a Tejana actor/writer/activist. She was featured on three seasons of "Russell Simmons Presents Def Poetry" on HBO, and on the NAACP Image Awards program on FOX. She is the creator of "Otra Esa on the Public Transit," a powerful one-woman stage show about destination and destiny, which she performed at San Antonio's Guadalupe Theater and Talento Bilingüe de Houston. She also stars in the award-winning independent film *Speeder Kills*, which was broadcast on SiTV and PBS. As a member of Chicano Messengers of Spoken Word, she co-wrote and performed the poetry/theater piece, "Fear of a Brown Planet," in San Francisco, Miami, Denver, and Houston. *Latina Magazine* honored Amalia for her role in founding, co-writing, directing, and performing in "Women of ILL Repute: Refute!" It was presented at the Texas Book Festival, Young Tongues Festival, San Antonio Inter-American Book Fair, Latina Letters Conference, Austin Poetry Festival, Austin Book Festival, and many universities.

Amalia Ortiz was the first Latina poet to ever reach the final round at the National Poetry Slam, where her team took the second place prize. She is a San Antonio Puro Slam three-time slam champion; an Open Slam Champion and Tag Team Champion (w/ Gary Mex Glazner) at the Taos Poetry Circus; and winner of the inaugural Ultimate Poetry Boxing Championship.

Ortiz's poetry is included on the spoken word compilations PoetCD.com, Sampler Vol. I, *NYC Urbana: the Very Best of 2003*, and *The Chicano Messengers of Spoken Word*. She participated in the Slam America National Bus Tour and is featured on the tour documentary "A Busload of Poets."

About the Cover Artist

Celeste De Luna is a painter/printmaker from Harlingen, Texas. She has exhibited her work in various cities in the Rio Grande Valley, San Antonio, San Diego, and Chicago. Of her work, Celeste writes: "My work is sometimes disturbing. The confluence of American and Xicano culture clash and sometimes harmonize in my work. My seemingly morbid interests go well with the death and despair of the border experience. Common themes in my work include migrant/border experiences of women, children, and families, the social effects of documentation status, and the spiritual struggle of conflicting identities, including 'survivor's guilt'."

You can see more of her work at www.celestedeluna.com.

Colophon

This first edition of *Rant. Chant. Chisme.*, by Amalia Ortiz, has been printed on 55 pound Edwards Brothers "natural" paper containing a percentage of recycled fiber. Titles have been set in Nueva type, the text in Adobe Caslon type. This book was designed by Bryce Milligan.

On-line catalogue and ordering:
www.wingspress.com
Wings Press titles are distributed to the trade by the
Independent Publishers Group
www.ipgbook.com
and in Europe by Gazelle
www.gazellebookservices.co.uk

Also available as an ebook.